The Story of
Our Lady of
Guadalupe

The Story of
Our Lady of Guadalupe

three people
four days
many miracles

by J. Janda

illustrated by
William Hart McNichols

Paulist Press New York/Mahwah

Photo of Our Lady of Guadalupe
courtesy of Maryknoll Missioners

Book design by Ellen Whitney

Text copyright © 1988 by J. Janda
Illustrations copyright © 1988 by William Hart McNichols

Library of Congress Cataloging-in-Publication Data

Janda, J. (James), 1936–
The story of Our Lady of Guadalupe: three people, four days, many miracles/by J. Janda: illustrations by William Hart McNichols. p. cm.
Summary: Retells the story of the miraculous appearance of Our Lady of Guadalupe to a humble Mexican Indian. Includes illustrations to color.
ISBN 0-8091-6573-2 (pbk.): $2.95 (est.)
1. Guadalupe, Our Lady of—Juvenile literature.
2. Mary, Blessed Virgin, Saint—Apparitions and miracles—Mexico—Gustavo A. Madero—Juvenile literature. [1. Guadalupe, Our Lady of. 2. Mary, Blessed Virgin, Saint—Apparitions and miracles. 3. Coloring books.] I. McNichols, William Hart, ill. II. Title.
BT660.G8J29 1988
232.91′7′097253—dc19 88-9784 CIP AC

Published by Paulist Press
997 Macarthur Boulevard
Mahwah, NJ 07430

Printed and bound in the
United States of America

For my nieces and nephews . . .

Kayla
and Brad

J. Janda

Justin
Chelsea
Meghan
Robert
Michael
Margie
Mary
Melissa
Meredith
and
Carry

W. McNichols

·▾·▲Preface▲·▾·

The story I am going to tell you is my favorite story. I heard it many times when I was a child, and later I read the same story in many different books. You see, many other writers and artists have also loved this story and made many books of words and pictures to tell it—each in his or her own way. It is the story of Our Lady of Guadalupe. I hope you enjoy reading it. I hope you have happy times coloring the pictures in this little book.

You can save this book. When you are older, you can read it again—or give it to a friend to show him or her the pictures you colored when you were young.

·▾·▲Three People▲·▾·

This story is about three people, four days, and many miracles—and so you must meet three people before the story begins, because it is all about them: Little John, Old John, and Bishop John.

·▾··▴ Little John ▴··▾·

Little John was short, not tall. He was a poor Indian. He planted corn and beans to eat. He would also pick fruit like prickly pears from the cactus. They tasted juicy and sweet. He would carry them home in his tilma.

All of the Indians had tilmas because they could be used for so many things. Mothers could wrap their babies in them to carry on their backs. Men could use them as sacks to carry fruit and vegetables home from the market—or when they were cold, they could wrap their tilmas around themselves to keep warm.

Little John was fifty-seven years old when this story begins. Because his wife had died, he was living with his uncle, Old John, because he liked him.

·▾·▲ Old John ▲·▾·

Old John was very happy that Little John moved in with him. He was always glad to see Little John when he came home from the fields. Old John would be waiting for him at the door and have a tasty meal of corn bread and hot beans all prepared. Old John's house was in the country, about nine miles from the city where Bishop John lived.

·▼·▲ Bishop John ▲·▼·

Bishop John was a good man, but he was often very sad because of the way the Spaniards were treating the Indians. You see, the Spaniards had just conquered Mexico. Many made slaves of the Indians and used to beat them.

Many Spanish people did not like Bishop John because he told them it was wrong to be cruel to the poor Indians. In the church he used to say, "God cries when you are cruel to anyone—especially the Indians." Some people would leave the church angry. They did not want to hear this.

And when Bishop John was alone, he used to pray to Mary, the mother of God. He would say, "O Mother Mary, bless the poor Indians, and teach the Spanish to be good to them. Send me some roses, Good Mother, so I will know you hear my prayers. And give us peace. Amen."

Bishop John lived in a big house in the city when this story begins.

·▾·▲ Four Days ▲·▾·

Now that you have met the three people—and where each lived—I will begin the story which all happened on four days: Saturday, Sunday, Monday, and Tuesday. It was a very early Saturday morning in December when the story begins.

·▾·▲ Saturday ▲·▾·

Little John was up very early. He looked out of the window and saw stars. He was getting ready to walk the long way to church because it was a special day when everyone prayed to God's mother. He dressed very quietly because his uncle, Old John, was not feeling well and he

did not want to wake him up. He put on his sandals, tiptoed out of the house, and then very quietly closed the door behind him.

It was dark outside, and cold, so Little John wrapped his tilma around himself to keep warm and then started walking. He followed the road he had taken so many times before: it led over and around the hills for many miles to the church.

It was also very quiet this morning. All that he heard was the sound of his sandals on the dry dirt road. All that he saw were the shapes of cactus and mesquite growing in the stony ground off the road.

But suddenly he heard music—like many birds singing. He looked around, but he could not see any birds. Then he saw a bright white cloud shining on the top of the hill. Then the edges of the cloud turned into all the colors of the rainbow. And then he heard a lady call his name.

He climbed the path to the top of the hill, and there he saw the most beautiful young Indian lady he had ever seen in his life. She had dark hair. Her long dress was rose-pink. Over her head and down to her feet was a big blue-green blanket and the edges were trimmed with gold, and on it were stars shining like gold.

And the birds kept singing, and the cactus shined like green emeralds, and the prickly pears glowed like purple jewels from the light around the lady. It looked as though she were standing in front of the sun. Then all was quiet and she spoke.

·▾··▲ The Lady Speaks ▲··▾· for the First Time

"Little Son," she said,
"I am Mary,
the mother of God
who made the stars and
the sky,
the sun and the moon—
this beautiful earth,
and each thing on it.

I have a favor
to ask of you.
Please go to Bishop
John
who lives in the city.

Tell him to build
a church for me
here in this valley.

Tell him that
I asked you to do
this for me.

I will be waiting here
for you when you come
back.
I want you then to tell
me
what Bishop John said."

·▾·▲ The First Visit ▲·▾· with Bishop John

Bishop John was a very busy man. He was planning to build schools for the Indians. And he had a lot of other things on his mind. Little John had to wait hours before he was allowed in. When a servant finally did lead him in, Bishop John listened carefully, but said, "Give me time to think about all of this. Come back in a few days."

Then the servant showed Little John out.

Little John's feelings were hurt because the bishop did not believe him. He was also sad because he had to tell God's mother what the bishop had said.

He slowly walked the many miles back to the hill, wondering what he would say. But as he reached the hill and started climbing the road up, he suddenly felt happy again. And there was the lady waiting for him, and she was smiling. She spoke.

·ᵛ·ᴬ The Lady Speaks ᴬ·ᵛ· a Second Time

"Little Son," she said,
"I know you feel sad
because the bishop
did not believe you.

Do not be afraid.
Do not worry
or be discouraged.

The bishop is testing
you.

He wants to be sure
that you are
telling the truth.

So please go to see him
again,
and tell him all

that I now tell you.

Tell him to build
a church here
in this valley
so people will
come to know me.

I am the mother of God
and your mother, too.

I am the mother of all
the people in the world.

I want all people to
know
that I listen to their
prayers
when they are sad.

I want all people to
know
that I love them
and will help them.

I want to take away
their sadness
and make them feel
happy again."

"I will try again, tomorrow," Little John
said. "Will you be here again?"

"Yes," the lady said.

"I wish," said Little John, "I wish you
would send someone else. I am just a poor Indian. I cannot read or write. Why are you send-
ing me?"

"Because I love you, because I trust you,"
she said.

"Go, Little Son.

I will be waiting for you here, tomorrow."

·▾·▲ Little John Returns Home ▲·▾·

So Little John returned home. Old John was not at the door to meet him. He went inside and found his uncle in bed.

"What is wrong?" Little John asked.

"It is nothing to worry about," said his uncle. "It's just that I don't feel too good. It will pass."

"Then I will make you something to eat," Little John said.

And while he was heating the beans over the fire, he noticed that his uncle was really too weak to get out of bed. When the beans were hot, he carried over a bowl of them and fed his sick uncle in bed.

And while Old John ate, he listened to all that Little John said, because Little John was telling him about everything that had happened that day.

And when his story had ended, he looked at his uncle and said, "But I don't think I should see the bishop tomorrow—while you are sick in bed."

"No," said the old man, "you must go."

"But what if you die?" Little John said.

"You must trust the lady and do as she said. Now go to bed. Leave early in the morning. Don't wake me up, but do as God's mother said."

So Little John went to bed and fell sound asleep as his uncle said.

·▼·▲ Sunday: Little John ▲·▼· Visits the Bishop

🌹 And early Sunday morning, Little John was on his way to visit the bishop again. Again he had to wait—this time, most of the day. Finally the servant again led him in to see the bishop. And again Little John told him all that the lady had said. And again the bishop listened carefully.

When Little John finished talking, Bishop John said, "Little John, you know I am a very busy man. If this lady is the mother of God, tell her I want a sign to prove it." (He didn't tell Little John—or anyone else for that matter—what the sign should be. In his own mind, he was thinking the sign should be roses—Castilian roses that grew only in Spain—even though it was winter in Mexico.)

Yes, Little John left and was discouraged. He really did not want to tell the lady that he had failed again. But again she was waiting on the hill for him, and for some reason he felt happy again.

·▾··▴ The Lady Speaks ▴··▾·
a Third Time

"Little Son," she said,
"I know the bishop
still does not believe
you.
I also know
that he asked you for a
sign,
a proof, that I really am
Mary,
the mother of God.

Tomorrow morning,
come back again.
I will give you a sign
to prove to the bishop
that I am the mother of
God,
and he will believe you.

He will build a church
for me
here in this valley
and all the people will
call me
Our Lady of
Guadalupe.

Go now, Little Son.
I know it has been a
long day
and that you are tired.

I will meet you here
tomorrow morning.
I will give the bishop
a sign."

·▼··▲ Little John Returns ▲·▼· Home Again

When Little John got home, his uncle could not get out of bed. He had a high fever. Even though Little John called in the Indian doctors, none of their medicines seemed to work. Little John was up all night watching his uncle and putting cold wet towels on his head. But by morning Old John grew worse.

·▼··▲ Monday ▲·▼·

On Monday morning, Old John could not get out of bed, he could not eat, and he could not speak. Little John stayed all day at his sick uncle's bed.

And that night, Little John was just falling asleep when his uncle said, "My nephew, I don't think I have much time left to live. In the morning, go to the city and bring me a priest to bless me and send my soul back to God."

"Oh, I will, my uncle, I will," Little John said.

·▾··▲ Tuesday ▲··▾·

And early Tuesday morning, Little John was walking as fast as he could to the city to do as his uncle had asked.

Suddenly, as he came near the hill where he had met the beautiful lady, he remembered what she had said. He also remembered that he had forgotten to return to see her as she had asked him to do.

He was feeling guilty about breaking his promise to her. He did not want to meet her again, so he took another road that led to the bottom of the hill.

Just as he was rounding the corner, there again stood the beautiful lady. And again she was smiling.

·▾··▲ The Lady Speaks ▲··▾· a Fourth Time

"Little Son, John,
where are you going?"
she asked.

He was very embarrassed, but said, "Dear Lady, I think my uncle is dying. I am going to get him a priest to bless him and send his soul back to God."

"That is not necessary," she said. "I have already saved your uncle's life. He is well. He will not die.

Go now to the top of the hill. There you will find the sign Bishop John asked for.

Bring me what you find."

So Little John started to climb to the top of the hill. As he was climbing up, he felt a warm spring breeze that smelled sweet like flowers— like roses. And at the top of that bare hill, where nothing would grow, were roses—Castilian roses, roses he had never seen before. With his little knife, he cut as many as he could carry in his tilma, then ran down the hill to the lady.

Although Little John was very excited, she was peaceful and kind. And as she carefully arranged the roses in his tilma, she said,

"Now you have a sign,
a proof, for the bishop.

Now he will believe
you.
Don't look sad;
he will believe you
this time.

He will build
the church for me here

and many people will
learn
that I am their mother
and that I wish to help
them
when they are lonely or
sad.

Go now, Little Son;
expect miracles and
you will find them."

·▾·▴ Little John Visits ▴·▾· the Bishop Again

Even though he had not slept much that night, he hurried all the way to Bishop John's house. He seemed to reach the house in no time. And soon he was led in to see the bishop again.

"My bishop," he said, "the lady gave me a sign."

He was so excited that he opened his tilma too fast and all the roses fell on the floor.

And then he saw Bishop John fall on his knees—not to look at the beautiful roses on the floor, but to stare at his tilma hanging open around his neck. For there on Little John's tilma was a perfect picture of the lady, just as he had seen her four times before.

(This picture has been photographed and can be seen all around the world—you can find a copy at the end of this book.)

·ᵥ·▲ Many Miracles ▲·ᵥ·

During the following days, many people heard about what had happened. So many good things were happening to Little John that he could not remember all of them.

He did return home to find his uncle, Old John, alive and well—and waiting for him at the door. Old John told him that after he had left for the priest, the beautiful lady had visited him and cured him.

Bishop John did build a church for the lady. Many Spaniards and Indians come to pray there and promise to respect each other and live in peace. Yes, Bishop John did receive his Castilian roses, in more ways than one.

And over the hundreds of years that have passed, many churches have been built in the valley where Little John first saw the beautiful lady, Mary, the mother of God. Yes, over the many years there have been changes, but one thing has not changed, and that is the picture on Little John's tilma. You can still see it today in Mexico City, in another new church for Our Lady of Guadalupe.

And remember, "Expect miracles and you will find them."